My Peace I Leave With You

To Dr. Bryan:
We are so blessed to have
your wealth of knowledge
as we care for our patients.
Peace is the goal of life.

Love
Vane

My Peace I Leave With You

The Peace Of God In Jesus Christ

Voice Guy

XULON PRESS

Xulon Press
2301 Lucien Way #415
Maitland, FL 32751
407.339.4217
www.xulonpress.com

Scripture quotations taken from the King James Version (KJV) – *public domain.*

Contributing informational sermons from Pastor Milton R. Hawkins,
Pentecostal Temple Church Of God In Christ.
Television Evangelists: Joel Olsteen, Joyce Meyers and T.D. Jakes
Pastor Alton R. Williams Of The World Overcomers Church
Random House Webster's Dictionary

Printed in the United States of America.

ISBN-13: 9781545679159

Dedication

This book is dedicated to God for Jesus Christ, and for my life. I am truly grateful for the inspiration that started me on this journey.

To my brilliant daughter, Dr. Carla Gillespie and my self-employed son, Michael Jones who are the very best of me.

To my grandchildren: Nahja, Philip, Hannah and Kayla. You are all a joy to me. A special thanks to Nahja for the technical assistance.

To my brother, Minister James A. Jones who has been a spiritual advisor, and is solely responsible for my initial spiritual education.

To my dear Aunt Theodora and Uncle Harry.

To Sandra Bradley for reading my first pages and giving feedback.

To the membership of Christian Unity M. B. Church and Mt. Herman A. M. E. Church.

To the group of classmates and friends from Hopkinsville, Ky. who I travel with yearly.

To the memory of my dear friend Jackie Coleman, who I miss daily.

Acknowledgement

Spiritual Advisors: *Minister James A. Jones, Pastor Eric Knowles, Pastor Linda Evans.*

Mt. Herman A. M. E. Church, Pastor Joy Wilkerson

Christian Unity Baptist Church, Pastor William Edwards

Endorsement

*Mount Herman A. M. E. Church Male Chorus who have supported
me for many years. I consider it a privilege to play piano for the
group. I believe that God chooses our journeys according to His
pleasure. I am grateful that God planted me with you.*

Table Of Contents

—◇◦⊙◦◇—

Introduction

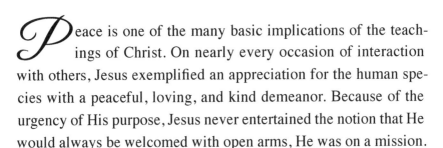

*P*eace is one of the many basic implications of the teachings of Christ. On nearly every occasion of interaction with others, Jesus exemplified an appreciation for the human species with a peaceful, loving, and kind demeanor. Because of the urgency of His purpose, Jesus never entertained the notion that He would always be welcomed with open arms, He was on a mission.

In John 5:41, Jesus said, "I receive not honor from men." He knew exactly what His mission was about. What He had to deliver was not meant to make anyone feel "warm and fuzzy." It was intended as a call to salvation for mankind. The Savior had come.

He had a goal to fulfill, which was first to capture the attention of as many people as He could. The second phase of Jesus' goal was as important as the first: lead those who were touched by His message to the fountain Of truth, and to eternal life. The truth was that God had designed explicit directions for Jesus' time on earth, and each Authoritative Dialectical was to be carried out just as it was outlined in God's plan.

The fulfillment of the Will Of God was Jesus' primary focus. John 11 reveals the story of Lazarus who had died four days earlier, Jesus raised him for the benefit of onlookers. He needed the witnesses to be direct recipients of the glory of God. Each act that

Jesus had performed among men was for the specific purpose of glorifying God.

Jesus displayed the peaceful attitude of grace and humbleness regardless of the circumstances. Based on the scriptures, there were times when situational assertions required Him to use different approaches to make a point, but the truth of the gospel was His primary determinant. The Bible records minimal instances of Jesus losing His temper. For instance, there was a time while visiting a synagogue, He was actually taken aback by people using The Father's House for buying and selling! "Saying unto them, it is written, My house is the house of prayer: but ye have made it a den of thieves." (Luke 19:46) He had to show them how distasteful this practice was, so He showed them in a way they could understand.

In spite of His usual calm manner, He was not readily trusted, and He was treated cruelly. He was misinterpreted, denied, despised, and apparently disrespected by those in power, who assumed that Jesus' appearance on the scene was a direct threat to their status on their scale of hierarchy. *A known carpenter's son who has come with the absurd assertion that He is on a personal assignment from God! Who does He think He is?* His countrymen, those whom He had grown up around, could not accept that Jesus could be the promised Messiah, so He alienated some of those who had been closest to Him, and His earthly family. In John 1:11, It is written, "He came unto His own, and His own received Him not."

It never seemed to matter to Jesus how He was mistreated or disregarded, He continued to be about the mission at hand, fulfilling the will of God. Jesus' ministry demonstrated for all of us, the perfect paradigm of peace and love. He had lived the definition of tolerance, patience, love, understanding and peace to impart to His followers that we are all made in the image and after the likeness of God, and therefore we possess the capability to love one another, and live in peace together, even with our multiple differences.

"My Peace I Leave With You"

Ephesians 2: 14-18

"For He is our peace, who hath broken down the middle wall of partition between us; having abolished in His flesh the enmity, even the law of commandments contained in ordinances; for to make in Himself of Twain one new man, so making peace; and that He might reconcile both unto God In one body by the cross, having slain the enmity thereby: and came and preached peace to you which were afar off, and to them that were nigh. For through Him we both have access by one Spirit unto the Father."

Peace Is Possible

*J*n spite of Jesus' demonstration of the perfect example, Peace has become an illusive concept for far too many people. Today, we have come to accept the horrors in life as commonplace, or "a sign of the times." Violence is viewed by some people as, "just the way it is. Today, the occurrences of the lack of peace in the world are more apparent, perhaps, because they are increasingly more visualized and more sensationalized. The more terrifying the events, the greater the audience, and the more horrifying the event, the greater the appeal. Many times, we as a society tend to condition ourselves to accept misconduct, terror and repugnance without the guilty being held accountable.

As Christians, we are to emulate the Spirit of Christ and stand up against wrong, no matter where it occurs. Responsibility is assigned based on the status of the involved parties, or as behaviors or beliefs of the past for some individuals, making it unappealing in our present state of existence, because things are different now. But are they really? In the book of Ecclesiastes 1:9, "The thing that hath been, it is that which shall be; and that which is done is that which shall be done: and there is no new thing under the sun." We live in a diverse society, some say, but is peace not a desired accomplishment for all aspects of human life? It is imperative that we do not fail to remember that God has not changed! In Malachi 3:6, "For I am the Lord, I change not."

All around us there is negativity, selfishness, betrayals, disappointment and disagreements. Perhaps bad news seems more obvious because information is transmitted more quickly, and the availability of broadcast news allows more instant reception. Thank God for the free press, but no matter how overwhelming it becomes, it provides us with information that we need to make informed decisions that affect our lives in many ways. Of course, the news media is the vortex responsible for the instantaneous transmission of events, and it is without a doubt the greatest source for our educational enlightenment concerning events around the world. It is incumbent on each one of us to filter our news intake, and keep our minds, hearts and souls in tune with the will of God to avoid the pitfalls of over-sensory stimulation.

The impact of confusion, rebellion and chaos in the human experience has been present in all definitions of relationships since the beginning of time. In Genesis 4:8, Cain slew Abel; in Genesis 6:5, God saw that every imagination of a man's heart was evil; and in Genesis 7:23, all living substance was destroyed from off the earth due to persistent disobedience and mankind's failure to allow the love and the peace of God to rule their lives.

God's Assurance In Time Of Trouble

a t one juncture, in a letter (recorded from God) delivered to the Children of Israel who were Babylonian captives at the time, Jeremiah stressed the necessity of maintaining peace among themselves. He encouraged them in Jeremiah 29:7, "And seek the peace of the city whither I (God) have caused you to be carried away captives, and pray unto the Lord for it: for in the peace thereof shall ye have peace." They were admonished to be content where they were, do all that they could to avoid conflict, and they were encouraged to make the best of an impossible situation because God was in control, and He would deliver them in due time. They were to follow the rules of the foreign land and not forget who they were to God. They were, after all, God's chosen people.

The Children Of Israel, of course knew exactly why they were being punished. God's intent for His prized possession was that they acknowledge that their disobedience had brought them into bondage. Their knowledge of His love for them should have been a determining factor in their remembrance that being in a foreign land did not negate God's promises to them. Through the Prophet Jeremiah, God was reaffirming His commitment to their well-being. He wanted to teach them important life lessons, and He wanted them to be cognizant of the reasons for His chastisement.

He expected their recognition that their survival depended on total reliance on His love.

God's plans for His people had been predestined long before any of them knew the importance of God's presence in their lives. In Jeremiah 29:11, "For I know the thoughts that I think toward you, saith the Lord, thoughts of peace, and not evil, to give you an expected end." The Israelites had been in various forms of bondage over the years, and God reminded them of His previous assurances to them, that He was still their God who would provide all of their needs. His love for them would make available for them everything that He had promised.

These events are just a few of the struggles and failures humans had suffered in an attempt to obtain peace in the world at that time, and sometimes it appears that not much has changed. The family population is more polarized and greater in number now, and we are better informed, but we too forget that God's Grace should be our motivation to respond to life's challenges in the faith that God is still here, and His Promises are just as valid.

We continue to deal with societal issues, including: sickness, disease, pain, death, despair, and assault manifested by human to human disrespect. Seemingly, occasions of anger, abuse, jealousy, enviousness, distrust, and sometimes, as some see it, apparently pure evilness, outweigh any semblance of peace.

The road to peace is paved with obstacles, but with faith in God, through Jesus Christ, the strongholds will be eradicated, because Jesus abolished that worry when He took the burden of all human suffering unto Himself as He voluntarily went to the cross. Jesus provided us with a solution to our problems by carving out a particular pathway to righteousness: HIMSELF!

Responding to one of His disciples, Thomas, who had asked how they could know the way to go if they did not know where He was going, Jesus replied in John 14:6, "I am the way, the truth, and the life:" Sincere faith and trust in Christ, opens appropriate doors and maps out for all believers purposeful guidelines for our journeys.

Humans have experienced difficulties and turmoil in one form or another for much of our existence, but peace is available to all of us who claim the privilege of living according to the standards that God initially established for us, such as in "The Ten Commandments." They were difficult to follow to the letter, but the commandment concept implies that in living by them, a certain peace will prevail. In Isaiah 48:18, "O that thou had hearkened to my commandments! Then had thy peace been as a river, and thy righteousness as the waves of the sea." The commandments are simply commonsense articles established to keep peace among human beings. They were specifically written as a commitment for man to God, and for man to man, (humankind.)

Sermon On The Mount

*W*hen Jesus began His ministry, cynicism was wide spread among the Pharisees and Sadducees. To set the record straight, He assured the disciples in Matthew 5:17, during His great Sermon on the Mount, "think not that I am come to destroy the law, or the prophets, I am not come to destroy but to fulfill." Jesus implored the disciples to consistently ensure the accuracy of His missionary message. The complete teaching of Matthew, chapter 5, details Jesus' fulfillment of the original commandments. He came to illuminate God's Grace and Mercy for mankind by providing a way to righteousness. Jesus came that mankind might enjoy the benefits of His steadfast love in peace and happiness, brought about through His sacrifice. Otherwise, His sacrifice would have been a gross waste of time. He would have laid His life down for absolutely nothing!

Pursuit Of Peace

*P*eace is definitely a worthwhile pursuit as a prerequisite to love. There can never really be real love without peace. When we love as God intended, peace is imminent. It should not be that difficult to achieve, when we strive to live by one very elementary concept, which is that we treat others as we would want to be treated. The love of Jesus transcends all types of barriers and it breaks through the glaciers of hatred and intolerance.

So, when I awoke one morning with my mind infused in the phrase, "my peace I leave with you," It gave me a sudden sense of delight that started me on a wondering journey. I could not shake the feeling as I pondered it's potential purpose. It stayed with me for the rest of the day and thereafter. It had to mean something, but what? Then, It occurred to me that I had read similar words before, in the Bible. I decided to read as many references to the word and to the concept of peace that I could find.

I found many.

I prayed for understanding and revelation for the constancy of my thought process regarding peace. I had no clue why this phrase persisted in my mind. I knew one thing: it had to have a purpose worth pursuing.

Going about my day, at one point, I began to hum the tune from a familiar hymn, from the National Baptist Hymnal, "What a friend we have in Jesus." A stanza relates, "Oh, what peace we often forfeit, oh, what needless pains we bear, all because we do not carry, everything to God in prayer." It became clearer to me why this song, one of many, had brought peace and contentment to the lives of many of our ancestors.

In my neighborhood, grandparents and parents frequently hummed familial songs as they performed various tasks. Apparently, these songs had provided them some degree of comfort and peace. It is certain that particular songs had brought solace to the souls of many. It is clear why the importance of the words in songs had been passed down through generations, and they never seem to grow tiring.

It is difficult to understand why anyone has to endure disrespect or inhuman treatment because of how they look or what their societal standing is. Most human beings are not interested in asking for handouts, they only want freedom and joy, to live a life of contentment, and they want to live in peaceful surroundings. Most people need to be free to express their opinions without reprisal or reproach.

Each person's needs are special to them, and should be respected as that individual's choice.

A Change

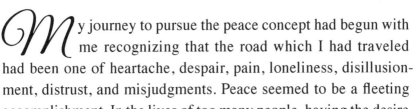

My journey to pursue the peace concept had begun with me recognizing that the road which I had traveled had been one of heartache, despair, pain, loneliness, disillusionment, distrust, and misjudgments. Peace seemed to be a fleeting accomplishment. In the lives of too many people, having the desire to work hard to achieve "The American Dream" was a foregone dilemma. Variable obstacles consumed every forward step, some deliberately set in their way, some circumstantial.

Implementations involved in maintaining the peace narrative are complicated and even perilous at times. In our individual lives, there are multiple considerations as to why peace appears unreachable. At other times outside influences prevail, like natural disasters, manmade incidents, in-home or institutional invasions; and other general intrusive impediments arise which can change the course of a perceived peaceful journey. Acts of perceived invasion that may interfere with the peace in select environments could include the situational neighborhood, the neighbors, friends, co-workers, family members and even total strangers. Any of these can become factors which deter the progress to a peaceful life.

I've spoken with individuals who had confided in me that it had become a chore to go out and enjoy a movie or dine with friends or family. Occasions that are supposed to be normal should not be that hard, some say. I have even spoken with many people who tell me that they are afraid to leave the house after dark, or they would love to go to a show or just go out for a jog, but the fear of being attacked, or worse, keeps them home.

2Timothy 1:7, "For God hath not given us the spirit of fear; but of power, and of love, and of a sound mind." One of the rationales for a sound mind is peace. Interaction with other humans is important for mind, body and soul strength. I believe that one of our main reasons for being is to love one another. We all have emotions, opinions, likes and dislikes, but we should be respectful of each other's point of view. Instead of getting angry when rejection occurs, we should learn to do as Jesus instructed the disciples in Matthew 10:14, "And whosoever shall not receive you, nor hear your words, when ye depart out of that house or city, shake off the dust of your feet." Obviously, Jesus was teaching about the delivery of The Gospel, but this advice works with other interactions as well.

It is not up to us to force anything on anybody. Christians are to compel lovingly and peacefully without judgement or harshness. It is important that we greet one another in the spirit of Christ. Every human being deserves dignity and respect. We are not to be the judge or jury that condemns anyone. Actually, Romans 12:19, "Dearly beloved, avenge not yourselves, but rather give place unto wrath: for it is written, Vengeance is mine; I will repay saith the Lord."

God calls to purpose

*G*od created the earth with humankind in mind, because He loved us, and wanted us to inhabit an atmosphere of peace, where we could thrive as we endeavored to do His will. He predestined each one of our roles on the world stage. I recall the words of Dr. Martin Luther King, Jr., "True peace is not merely absence of tension, it is the presence of justice." While advocating for equal rights, Dr. King never gave up on the mission he was convinced was assigned to him. His vision was to fight for justice, for all people.

The Discovery

*I*n December 2002, my heart was led to seek a higher calling, and discover more meaning for my life. I started by accepting an invitation to a church where I eventually found an answer. My brother, a pastor at the time, had invited me to his church. I went. I needed a breakthrough, a spiritual renewal. I got that, and more, and I have not looked back. The first sermon that I heard on my return to church was about the Apostle Paul. He announced himself as "the chiefest of sinners." Hearing Paul's story gave me the bold determination to seek my purpose, and it inspired me to listen intently for what the Lord would say to me. I realized that if God used Paul to deliver His message, why not me? It was this realization that provided me the opportunity to vigorously pursue that higher calling, so with the guidance of the Holy Spirit I began to write plays and speeches for church occasions. I was inspired to learn to play piano and sing. At first, when the inclination pricked my heart, my response was, excuses! "I'm too old, I can't do that, I do not have the time," or anything to convince myself why I should not proceed. working in the church has been my spiritual endowment. I thank God for this awesome responsibility of writing, from His Heart to mine.

Sacrifice Of Christ

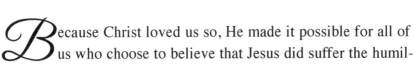

*B*ecause Christ loved us so, He made it possible for all of us who choose to believe that Jesus did suffer the humiliation, shame and torture of the cross. He suffered to give us the chance to experience the joy of a more abundant life. Through our belief, ZZHe made possible the opportunity for a life of peace.

Our peace comes with having the assurance that Christ is our Redeemer. For mankind to achieve the peace of Christ, we must be cognizant of His sacrifice. The knowledge that Christ is our Savior makes it possible for mankind to have the wisdom to understand that, because He loves all mankind, He created a pathway for all non-Jews to be accepted into the will of God. Our peace is dependent on the sacrifice of Christ's life. If He had not given His life, we would have no reason to pursue eternal life in Christ. We achieve peace in our faith in God through the love of Jesus, recognizing that God, and God alone, is the Master Manipulator of His creation.

Throughout the Old Testament, peace offerings were made part of the customary, traditional acts of the God-required first fruits of animal and plant harvests. These first-fruits were to be submitted to God by the people of God for specific purposes. These strict rituals were instituted by God to the people, and done to ultimately show allegiance to God. The rituals also provided a road map for the journey of the people of God to travel, so that they fully recognized and appreciated the Sovereignty of the only Living God, and accepted Him as the Divine Benefactor on whom they could totally depend.

Peace is primarily a state of satisfaction in realizing our ability to function freely and effectively to achieve specific goals without fear or shame. Peace allows us to have the confidence to maintain a positive attitude in spite of environmental interferences, and it is the necessary component in having peace of mind, where we can consistently feel the joy of the Lord in our heart. Peace is defined in *Random House Webster's Dictionary* as freedom from war, trouble or disturbance.

When considering the art of peace, and the difficulty we face in achieving it, it seems like a no-brainer to me that we can truly live and thrive together in peace, if we take the time to remember the sacrifice of Jesus Christ. The vision of this concept reveals to me that humans are capable of experiencing wholesome lives by consciously exercising the act of reciprocity in respecting the rights of one another.

If we believe in The Savior for the whole world, it should not be a dubious undertaking acknowledging that Jesus has to be the source of all joy, hope, love, peace, happiness, and all other good things in life. In the book of Matthew 24:6, Jesus said, "And ye shall hear of wars and rumors of wars: see that ye be not troubled:" In fact, in the midst of troubles, when we foster peace in Jesus Christ, He will sustain us. Our confidence in Jesus Christ should be the catalyst to our peace of mind. We only need a minute "mustard seed" measure of faith to believe that He has given us full authority to call on His name when we are in trouble, when we are coming out of trouble, and when there is perceived anticipation of entering into trouble. Jesus did all that He did for our benefit. He really does want us to trust in His Lordship. All we need to do is believe that He is the promised Lord Of Lords!

Peace And The Books Of The Bible

One day as I watched television, I learned from a well-known evangelist, that peace is used over 400 times in the sixty-six books of the Bible. In my research, I found every book of the Old Testament exemplifies the concept of peace, except Ruth, Song Of Solomon, Hosea, Joel and Habakkuk. And every book of the New Testament, except 1John.

It is reasonable to believe that peace is one of many important life concepts for the Christian, as well as the non- Christian. It is that part of any human's well-being to seek a life of happiness and enjoyment of God's awesome creation. Performing worthwhile tasks outside of a conducive environment that inspires critical focus and clarity is difficult. Peace is necessary to achieve the spiritual mind-fulness required to obtain the self-assurance needed to relate to one another, and most assuredly, to commune with God. We must be open to hearing the voice of God. As stated in Matthew 26:41, "The Spirit is willing, but the flesh is weak." At one particular time, Jesus had asked the disciples to watch for an hour while He went away to pray, but when He returned they were asleep. Jesus understood that the disciples were willing, but they were human.

To focus and redirect our minds to God's Will, we must be awake, we must be spiritually and mentally adaptable, and we must be open to receiving what the Lord has already predestinated for us, which will not be achievable without peace. "God's Word" is our standard for being, and therefore must be considered our "standard for an abundant life." On the other hand, it probably would have been fruitless to inspire the term "peace" as much in the Bible. The term peace would not have been included in all but six books of the Bible, if it had not been important, and had it not been possible for us to achieve. Jesus portrayed the greatest example for us by voluntarily coming to earth in human form, humble and lowly, just like most of us. Ordinarily humans do not come into the world established and needing nothing. Quite the contrary. Had Jesus come any other way, I believe that His presence would not have been as effective.

The Disciples' Preparation

———————◇◦⬳◦◇———————

*J*esus' spoken words prior to and after His crucifixion were to be consolation for the world. Before His death, Jesus was apparently preparing the disciples for His expected departure, and to leave with them His peaceful assurance. It was near the completion of His divine mission on earth, and Jesus had to condition the disciples' minds to accept with surety that He would no longer be with them in human form. He had to go away. It was important that the disciples fully recognize the necessary applications for what they would be expected to do, and also imperative that they be confident in their ability to exercise what they had learned through their close relationship with Him. To be effective in the delivery of the Gospel, the disciples would need to present what they had learned in a way that would compel those of us who were to come that what they taught was indeed the good news from "The Ultimate Teacher."

Jesus had taught the disciples so they could figure out the answers to problems for themselves by recalling His example. He had taught them using parables so they could grasp the meaning more clearly. There education consisted of explicit, detailed instructions, necessary to ensure their readiness for carrying out their missions. Jesus had specifically chosen each of the disciples for this important journey by showing them how to appreciate each and every interaction with multiple individuals and groups. Jesus stressed the importance of understanding that all experiences of interaction should be taken as unique opportunities for growth, and for the development of their ability to scrutinize and critically observe various aspects of human behavior.

Jesus was no respecter of persons when it came to meeting people where they were, or when it came to the delivery of His message. Any one who was willing to give and receive was welcome. He wanted each disciple to achieve this level of maturity because it would be crucial to them on their journeys. They had received first hand knowledge through accompanying Jesus on each phase of His earthly mission. Jesus needed them to mirror what they had seen in Him, and He needed them to perform their work with boldness.

Jesus never wavered in His mission. He kept the goal of His mission in the front of His mind, "accomplishing the will of God." He chose the disciples for a special purpose: To sufficiently capture what they had learned, and to utilize that ability to direct and teach others "in the way of the Master." They had been taught to have confidence in their ability, and to be astute in recalling the instructions they had been taught. Jesus knew that these skills would be required in order for them to enlighten all of those who accepted the challenge to follow His teachings.

An integral requirement of Jesus' ministry was that whoever showed interest in His teaching be given the opportunity to receive the basic intention of the gospel: to believe in faith that Jesus Christ is Lord and, through Him, receive salvation, and lead others to understand Jesus' profound impact for the world. He needed the disciples, and us, to receive the basics, and, build on what we learned to help those who would come after us.

It was important to Jesus that we take care of one another, and most especially the poor, the sick, and the weakest among us. Jesus used multiple methods of instruction to engage the disciples in the process of gaining a complete grasp of what He needed them to know. He used parables as described in the synoptic books of the New Testament. God had previously inspired Prophets like Isaiah, Ezekiel, and Jeremiah, messengers and servants like Job, Moses and Abraham to reveal His message of love and peace throughout the Old Testament. It's all about love. Our lives are based on the love and peace of God.

The disciples would need to use what they had learned independent of Jesus' personal guidance and physical presence. Jesus had to go away soon. They would be on their own, but with a very present help, the directive of the Holy Spirit, to set, encourage and manage their paths as they performed their duties. They were picked because of who they were when Jesus chose them, "Workers."

We, too, need to be about The Father's business. When we pursue our designed purpose, we travel a refined line of love, contentment, joy and, equally important, peace, which comes with trust in the knowledge and acceptance of God's Amazing Grace. Jesus had critically and lovingly studied each of the disciples and knew exactly how they would perform and what He could expect from them. He had intimately studied each one's heart, character, personality, and willingness to adapt to follow the plan to fulfill

God's will, while following His leadership. He wanted the disciples to have faith in themselves and recognize that they had everything they needed to succeed. After all, they had been trained by The Lord. They only needed the confidence in their ability to maximize the teaching they had received.

The disciples were not unlike humans today. They acknowledged their difficulty in believing that they were in personal contact with the Lord. Yes, they questioned His authority, yes, they questioned who Jesus was. Even His cousin John asked at a vulnerable period, while imprisoned, "are you the One?" John had asked the question even though he had earlier announced Jesus' credibility as he baptized Him. They knew that this Teacher was different, that He spoke with personal knowledge that they had never experienced from any teacher before, yet they had doubts. It would be difficult for any of us to believe that we are in the divine physical presence of the Lord. Jesus had been here in a human form that resembled our own. He actually walked among the people with specific goals: To demonstrate for us the concept of LOVE. To reveal to the world that humans really can live a peaceful existence by following His path to victory, established by Our Heavenly Father! All that we need is faith to believe, and understand that even that allotted small measure of faith would be tested again and again.

Jesus had to humanize Himself to make assessments based on an ordinary man's understanding. It was imperative for the disciples' growth that Jesus analyze each of them this way. They needed to utilize the effective learning tools from the perspective of divine wisdom. It was necessary for them to develop sufficiently to carry out the mission on which they were about to embark.

Jesus formed His assessments from His human mindset so the disciples could know just how possible it would be for them. He is calling on us to do the same, because as Philippians 4:13 says, "I can do all things through Christ which strengtheneth me." The assessments were initially made from dual perspectives. The messages were based on Jesus' 100 percent spiritual perspective, and delivered from His 100 percent human perspective. He revealed heavenly expectations, that had to be received by human mentalities. Jesus was on a divine mission that had to be delivered in a relatively short period of time. This had to be done from His Human perspective for the message to be conducive for earthly human consumption. He instructed the disciples in Matthew 28:19, "Go ye therefore, and teach all nations, baptizing them in the name of the Father, and of the Son, and of the Holy Ghost:" as He had taught them. And, in addition, He specifically implied to them that they always do so peacefully, and in love.

The woman at the well in John chapter 4 was inspired by Jesus' concern for her well being, even though Jews and Samaritans rarely interacted on a regular basis. Jesus spoke to her without malice or disdain because He wanted her to have the opportunity to be a better version of who she was. Jesus had made each encounter, regardless of the situation, a love-instructed opportunity. He wanted peace among all nations. It was part of Jesus' love inspired mission. He knew that the disciples had witnessed all that he had done, but He also knew that their humanness would sometimes be a major obstacle to reaching their God-defined goals. The disciples were confused by Jesus' attitude toward the woman. Wasting precious time with Samaritans was not an accepted practice among the general population of Jews of that day.

The disciples could not understand why Jesus wanted to leave, but He impressed upon them how fruitful it would be for them, that He go away. If He did not go away, they would not receive the guidance of the Holy Spirit. They would not receive the blessing of the Holy Spirit to lead them in the fullness of their time. They had to be the bold champions Jesus knew they could be. And, most importantly, this step was all part of God's plan.

The Divine Plan

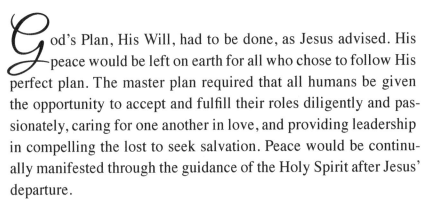

God's Plan, His Will, had to be done, as Jesus advised. His peace would be left on earth for all who chose to follow His perfect plan. The master plan required that all humans be given the opportunity to accept and fulfill their roles diligently and passionately, caring for one another in love, and providing leadership in compelling the lost to seek salvation. Peace would be continually manifested through the guidance of the Holy Spirit after Jesus' departure.

The plan for our lives was established by Christ to afford us the gift of life in choosing the peace of "God's Amazing Love" as we work to reach our goal of eternal life. Matthew 22:36-39, Jesus answered a lawyer who attempted to tempt Him when he asked, "Master, which is the great commandment in the law?" Jesus simply restated from the law, "thou shalt love the Lord thy God with all thy heart, and with all thy soul, and with all thy mind. This is the first and great commandment. And the second is like unto it thou shalt love thy neighbor as thyself."

There can be no love without peace . One of the main ingredients for a wholesome life, after love, is PEACE, along with each of the components of the "Fruit Of The Spirit" as defined in Ephesians 5:9, and is found in all "goodness, righteousness and truth." This peace is only achieved through Christ Jesus. In the book of Romans

5:1, "Therefore being justified by faith, we have peace with God through our Lord Jesus Christ." Peace and love are spiritually determined and inherent in all of us, and are to be demonstrated one to another. Showing love for one another is the only way we can outwardly express our understanding of God's expectation for the peace of mankind. We can not impress God with love for Him if we can not express love for our fellow man.

When we love one another, we express our understanding of God's love for us.

Because God knows our hearts, it is impossible to conceal the truth of who God already knows each of us to be. However, it is sometimes easy for us to deceive one another with worthless phrases that are used to stroke our personal egos, or to influence those around us. When we genuinely care for one another, then there is no pretense. We will only need to be who God made us to be, servants of The Most High.

If we truly understand that it was God's pleasure to create us for His divine purpose, we can enjoy our lives in peace. Philippians 4:7, "And the peace of God, which passeth all understanding, shall keep your hearts and minds through Christ."

God's Justice

—◇○⟨⟨⟩⟩○◇—

*W*e can live in the knowledge of truth and justice, using the same principles to relate to every person. Real justice is meeting every one in the same manner, by applying the same God-directed principles. From the heart we justify each other. Jesus is the perfect example of who we can be. If He is the Head of our lives, we should expect this same example from every one we encounter. When examples of goodness and peace are exercised in individual families, it should not be difficult to apply the same standards and principles in all aspects of our lives. No pretense needed, but doing all things to the Glory Of God.

Jesus said in the gospel of Matthew 6:2, "Therefore when thou doest thine alms, do not sound a trumpet before thee, as the hypocrites do in the synagogues and in the streets, that they may have glory of men." If we remember to show the same dignity and respect to everyone at all times, we will not fail to be encompassed with the fullness of the Glory of God.

Glory from men is usually conditional, and often provides only instant gratification. In order to achieve the abundance of true love, joy, peace, happiness and all of the other components of the "Fruit Of The Spirit," we must be open and willing. We can accomplish our heart's understanding of "The Fruit Of The Spirit" conceptually, when we allow the Spirit of God to direct our hearts. They work together to form a complete standard of love in peace. It is important to note, "The Fruit Of The Spirit" is written as a singular, "Fruit," but further reading in Galatian 5:22-23, implies it is impossible to achieve the concept independently. It must be present in each heart as a whole, understanding that it is difficult to display one without the other.

A Dream?

I awoke one morning with a dreamt phrase still in my head: "My Peace I Leave With You." I could not dismiss it. I thought about the phrase throughout my morning ritual, and It stayed with me as I continued my day. The phrase was in my head for the rest of that day and for multiple days thereafter. I had to acknowledge that this phrase pursued my thoughts for a reason. It became clear to me as I earnestly considered the matter that something was happening, and I questioned the purpose why I was led to keep this phrase on my mind, "My Peace I Leave With You." It was as though Jesus spoke to my heart, "My peace has always been with you. It is to be used for the purpose for which I will lead you."

I remembered an incident that occurred when I was a child, that I thought I had forgotten. I actually tried to forget it. But here it was breaking into my conscious thoughts.

It was late one evening when I slipped into bed between the coolness of the sheets. It is difficult for me to recall what time of the year it was, or why I happened to be the only kid awake, but as I lay in bed, I was overcome by this presence. I tried to move, I could not. I even tried to blink my eyes, I could not. Then it happened. I saw, standing at the foot of my bed a figure draped in glowing white, almost like a halo that completely encircled the figure. It was not a frightening experience, because this was a calm, peaceful presence. I was young, I'm guessing, maybe 10 years old. I am not sure how long the figure remained, but the minute I regained my faculties, I jumped out of bed, and walked quickly to the kitchen where grandmother was cooking. When she asked, why I was out of bed, I can recall that I lied. I was afraid to tell her what really happened. I probably mumbled something else that I can not remember. I do know that I did not tell her the truth about what I had experienced.

To this day I have not discussed the incident seriously with anyone. Trying to forget about it has not been easy. It has been anxiety- provoking, because I was more concerned that people would think that I was a nut, rather than consider what the purpose was. I've never been able to figure out the reason for the appearance, but I do know that I am waiting and praying for the answer. I imagine that I will know the purpose in due time. It was such a comforting experience that it could not have been meant for evil.

Was it a dream? I do not know. I do know that nothing would please me more than to finally have an explanation. I believe that I can now handle the revelation when it comes.

We are all blessed by God to bless someone else for some purpose. Because the "peace" phrase stayed in the forefront of my thoughts, I realized along the course of the day that Jesus was perhaps reminding me that these words were relevant today, and important for our missions as children of God. John 21:21, Jesus appeared to the disciples after the resurrection reminding them again, "peace be unto you: as my Father hath sent me, even so I send you." Matthew 6:9, "Blessed are the peacemakers for they shall be called the children of God." We are to be peace ambassadors for one another. The "BE" attitudes from Matthew 5:3-11, are definitely additional Commandments for our fullness of life. In addition, they are Jesus' message of the fulfillment of the law.

As I continued to ponder the "My Peace I Leave With You" phrase, and the answer, I felt strengthened and empowered. I had

to conclude that this revelation meant something, and I was determined to seek the answer to my mind's preoccupation with the
phrase, and for what purpose it served.

Trust In The Lord

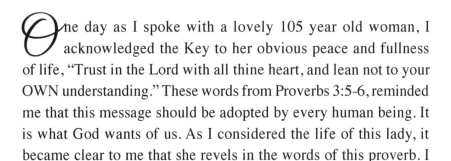

*O*ne day as I spoke with a lovely 105 year old woman, I acknowledged the Key to her obvious peace and fullness of life, "Trust in the Lord with all thine heart, and lean not to your OWN understanding." These words from Proverbs 3:5-6, reminded me that this message should be adopted by every human being. It is what God wants of us. As I considered the life of this lady, it became clear to me that she revels in the words of this proverb. I am convinced that her trust in God has preserved her wisdom and knowledge to impart to others the amazing strength of God's word.

She apparently lives her life based on her understanding of the inspiring word of God. I believe that her heart holds tightly to the concept that God truly is exactly who He says He is.

Another scripture Matthew 6:33, says, "But seek ye first the Kingdom of God, and His righteousness; and all these things shall be added unto you." In other words, when we find God, and understand our purpose as designated by Him, peace is inevitable. It is simply a matter of choice, understanding that all our needs will be provided as we work toward achieving a closer relationship with "The One" who sustains us in life.

When Solomon says in Proverbs 3:5-6, "Trust in the Lord with all thine heart and lean not to your own understanding," he reminds us that God's love dictates what He expects of us. He wants us to fully rely on Him for all that we do in life, because He is in control of all things and our trust in Him will yield benefits for a full, happy, joyful, peaceful and tranquil life.

Holy Spirit Leadership

When Jesus left, He promised us a great gift, a Comforter to cushion and condition all of life's challenges. We can never fail as we allow the Holy Spirit's leadership to guide us, body, mind and soul. Receiving the Holy Spirit into our lives greatly enhances our livelihood and produces outcomes which insures that we achieve all perspective purposes as designed by our Father, GOD. Our purpose can only be accomplished if we trust in Him!

Reckoning

---— ⋄⋗⫯⫯⋖⋄ ---—

$\mathcal{I}$t has taken some of us years to understand that all human lives have a purpose from the foundation of the world. There are people who I've met along my life's journey who actually believed that they were worthless, with no hope. There were times when obstacles along their paths caused distractions, and had them believe that love, joy, and, especially peace, were merely episodes of oblivion that some one else experienced. But, not so. God intends a peaceful, loving, prosperous life for all mankind.

God's intent for human beings is that we support one another in all that we strive for, and do so in love. Sometimes it is easier to keep our innermost thoughts to ourselves to avoid the risk of being judged unfavorably. When we think that this is the best choice, it is probably not a good idea, because the various aspects of our lives exist to educate either ourselves or someone else. It is difficult, but none of us should ever be caught up in the web of confusion about what others think of us, rather than in the web of love and peace where Jesus welcomes us completely in to God's Grace.

In God's service, He employs no bias in regard to race, gender, or any other variable that humans use to restrict each other. Stranger still, why do we limit God? God will shower His blessings on us wherever we are. He has already predestined every one of His children for a role in the upkeep of the kingdom. He is the source of life in all human beings, who should desire the achievement of peace with gladness and joy.

Some, like me, had determined that prior life experiences had consisted of a series of failures and disappointments, so there was no hope of measuring up to God's standards. What a huge mistake! An encounter with the ultimate "peacemaker" shone a light brightly on and changed the path of my history. No one can begin to understand another's struggle unless they have walked the same road. Everyone is looking for validation for who they really are. The many mistakes and missteps along the way are merely errors of maturing, leading to renewed growth. They are the steps to accomplishing our purposes for life. I learned from every mistake and horrible decision, the hard way, and I am thankful for the growth and wisdom that I gained traveling the broad road of life. Traveling the narrow road has proven to be the highway to peace.

Source Of Strength

───◦○❧○◦───

*N*ot until I found the source of my strength did everything began to come together. There is so much capability in each and every one of us. We only need to recognize that God chose us from the "foundation of the world" for a purpose. I am able to live in peace because of Jesus Christ, who showed up in my life and revealed the truth of who I am to Him.

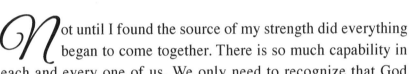

The Master's Plan

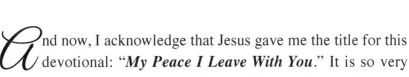

*A*nd now, I acknowledge that Jesus gave me the title for this devotional: *"**My Peace I Leave With You**."* It is so very clear for me. Many of us struggle with the question, "why was I chosen to suffer?" I have decided that it was because Jesus, without a doubt, has been with His chosen from the beginning of our individual journey which started at birth. We are chosen by God to be nurtured and matured into who He ordains us to be. It is an enlightening experience to know that I am a part of the "Master's Plan!" To fully appreciate the guidance of Almighty God, we must be molded and shaped in a fashion to be used by God. This process takes time.

Jesus came to earth to teach us the most peaceful, perfect way to live, but before He left, He made it a point to train the disciples to go, teach, and preach without fear because, "My Peace will be with you." This message is just as valid today as during the disciples time, and I pray that this devotional will help someone along their life's journey.

This devotional provides guidance from several scriptural formulas for every month, for an entire year. It is the purpose of God's Word to provide us with the peace of God's intent. You will find such peace in the joy of the Lord! May God bless you and keep you. Amen.

Devotional For
Each Month Of The Year

January

Genesis2:8, "And the Lord God planted a garden eastward in Eden; and there He put the man whom He had formed."

God's intent for us: The purpose for man from the beginning was to live in peace under the protection of God.

When God chose to create the world, it was with humans in mind. There was no "Big Bang!" involved in "THE GOD Creation" but, something more profound. God's intent for mankind was for us to live a pre-determined peaceful existence in a pre-established peaceful environment. The world was created in the immeasurable Love of God specifically for His proposed greatest creation: human beings. He carved out a place for man to grow and thrive as His magnificent masterpiece. He knew that for man to effectively appreciate the extent of His love, we would need to be in the image and likeness of Himself.

Human beings were created to continue the Kingdom building process. God knew that we would need the capabilities of reason and wisdom to succeed in our God-designated roles. God knew we would require the appropriate mental and physical abilities to make objects from things that He had created. He knew we would need the gift of interaction with other humans who could give and receive from a mutual perspective. God knew all of this, yet He gave us the freedom to find the answers for ourselves, and from others who would dwell in the same space where He placed us.

The love that began the creation is the same love God employs with the human race today. This love fest began because God wanted man to receive His grace freely, and appreciate His great plan for our lives. His goal for all human beings is that we enjoy the life that He chose to establish just for us, His master creation. Adam and Eve were positioned in the garden of Eden as God's prized possession, were entrusted with caring for all that was created. They failed in maintaining their trust in God. They were led astray by a serpent, of all things!

This failure revealed man's ability to color outside the lines of God's established domain. God knew of course, that humans would need the assurance of His Grace for a peaceful existence among other brothers and sisters. He knew that challenges would arise in life, which would turn humans' attention away from Him. God so wanted an extension of Himself, one that would be willing to accept His Divine Wisdom and follow His precepts for life on earth. He supplied all that we need to have the kind of existence He prepared for us.

We must acknowledge that humankind has never had to actually create anything; but, we simply make various objects from previously God-created things. He provided us a place to carry out His will for our lives. The sun shines whether we are happy or sad. The rain pours on us whether we need it or not. Everything works in concert to maintain just the right balance for everyday human life. The world is perfect as God created it, and all that is required of man is to care for what God has placed us in charge of: "The Kingdom here on earth." There is no doubt that if God did not love His master creation, then life as we know it would never have been an absolute in God's Heart. More profoundly, we would never be. It was God's desire that we have all that we need to prosper in the life that He has given us.

God's love for us is continuously Omnipotent (Almighty), Omnipresent (Everywhere at the same time), and Omniscient (All knowing), evidenced by the fact that He created an environment from nothing where human beings can prosper and enjoy the peace of His everlasting protection. Not select persons, but each of us enjoys the benefits of God's perfected peace and love. He could have provided the select environment for the select few, but because He never fails in His love, He is continuously all around, and He knows exactly who we are. He is in charge of the universe, but He allows man to run the day to day activities.

February

Genesis1:26, "And God said, let us make man in our image, and after our likeness:"

It was God's choice to love us: God's love and His peace for mankind.

Animals were made distinctly in a God-designed animal-image. However, the unmatchable wisdom of God dictated that man be made in His image and after His likeness. It is clear to this writer that God chose us as the superior creation because we *are* made in His image and after His likeness. He is The Superior God. If God had created us in any other image or likened us to any thing else, then we could not have been His "chosen ones." God's choice of mankind as master race is specific and, for each of us, should be gratifying. Profoundly, we should face the reality that God could have chosen any other species as His executor on earth. He can do what ever He wants, but He chose man as His master creation. He wanted us to realize His intentions for us, which was to accept Him as our God, and with this acceptance, follow the principles and guidelines that He established for us to continue the work of building His kingdom. We are supposed to peacefully work together in the upkeep of the Kingdom of God. He sent us a Savior for just that purpose. When Jesus came to earth, it was with the understanding that mankind would eagerly receive Him as Lord and follow the precepts that He had demonstrated. He came to show us a more peaceful way to come together.

God chose many servants prior to sending His Only Son. His chosen servants, "mere men," were picked because of their level of obedience to the "Word of God" and because they possessed an innate spiritual knowledge that God is Lord of all. It should not be any different among humans today. God has delineated the task of speaking on His behalf to preachers, teachers and others who share the love of the gospel. Despite that love, they simply could not meet the challenge of being the Savior, Comforter, Lord Of Lords, King of Kings, Counselor, and specifically, Redeemer or Lamb of God, because of various human frailties. God had to come in human form to show us that being made in His image and after His likeness, we can emulate His love among our brothers and sisters as children of God.

There was only One who could fulfill the awesome task of reconciling mankind in the love and peace of God: Jesus Christ!

March

Genesis 2:15, "And The Lord God took the man, and put him into the garden of Eden to dress it and keep it."

His Divine Plan: God's major intent for mankind to work together in peace and to love one another.

God chose man to be the keeper of His creation! He placed confidence in the man, made in His image, and after His likeness, to be an extension of Himself. We are His love interest!

God created the universe! God created man, placed him in the position of overseer, protectionist and nurturer of the human species to teach the precepts and commandments for life in love, joy, peace and contentment. He wanted us to have the satisfaction of knowing that He would never leave us. All that God wanted of us was to be completely obedient to Him, as Lord. The apparent expectation is that, since God made a special place for us to thrive and grow in His grace, then man would have no problem reciprocating. God loves us, and we should love God. The greatest commandments is to "love the Lord with all our heart, mind and soul," and the second greatest is to "love our neighbor as ourselves."

The Bible is very explicit in detailing the concept of LOVE. In love, life is beautiful, joyous, and kind. As God prepared our hearts to receive love and care for one another, He expected us to love and care for all human beings. Every single detail of God's Creation was completed with man in mind. Throughout the Bible, love is the major component of God's actions toward human beings. In Deuteronomy 10:17, "For the Lord your God is God of gods, and Lord of lords, a mighty, and a terrible, which regardeth not persons, nor taketh rewards." The love of God should be reciprocal: just as God loves us, we should love Him.

It does not matter to God what the race, creed, or color of people. He is no respecter of persons. Make no mistake, God loves all of us equally, and He does it for no charge. His love is unconditional, otherwise, how can we explain the rain on the just as well as the unjust? The opportunity to receive the blessing of The Savior is open to anyone regardless of status: rich and poor, black and white, male and female, educated and laymen. The door opens to all the same way. Sunshine is supplied to every one on the same level. No one is exempt. When the sun shines, there is no discrimination. There are many examples of God's Love for all. Wouldn't you agree?

April

Genesis 2:19, "And out of the ground the Lord God formed every beast of the field, and every fowl of the air; and brought them unto Adam to see what he would call them: and whatsoever Adam called every living creature, that was the name thereof."

Dominion: mankind's God designated responsibility. God desired all His creation to live together in peace.

When this universe was created, God placed people, those who He had chosen, to worship Him. Our roles were predestined before the foundation of the world, long before any thing was brought into existence. He had determined what each of us would bring to the table, as it related to our role in the kingdom of God. The trials we would suffer, the mistakes we would make, the length of time it would take each of us to mature into our roles. Everything about us was known by God long before we knew who we were.

Amazingly, God continues to direct us through the power of the Holy Spirit. Psalm 23:3, "He leaded me in the paths of righteousness for His Name's sake." He desires us to live up to His image and mimic His ways. For us to travel in a God-designated peaceful line, we must recognize that without God on our side, we would run off course, or crash and burn. What other explanation could there be for the many perilous encounters that we surely escape on a daily basis? Detours and disasters happen to people every single day. "why couldn't that have happened to me?" should be the question to ask ourselves, individually as well as collectively.

As with Adam and Eve, our roles are also determined. Adam and Eve failed by disobeying the will of God. He expected complete reliance on Him for all things. In Genesis 2:16-17, "And the Lord God commanded the man, saying, of every tree of the garden thou Mayest eat." "But of the tree of the knowledge of good and evil, thou shalt not eat of it: for in the day that thou eatest thereof thou shalt surely die." We only need the understanding of God's intent for His responsible servants. When we are willing to receive then we can perform accordingly.

In Psalms 8:6, God placed all things in man's hand for the purpose of nurturing and protecting what He had created. Verse 6 states, "Thou madest Him to have dominion over the works of thy hands: thou hast put all things under his feet:" we are trusted by Almighty God to care for all creation! An awesome responsibility, but imagine the benefits of God's Love for mankind.

May

Genesis 4:9-10, "And The Lord said unto Cain, where is Abel thy brother? And he said, I know not: Am I My brother's keeper? And He said, "what hast thou done? The voice Of thy brother's blood cruelty unto me from the ground."

We really are our brother's keeper: Caring for one another is who we are to be.

God does intend for us to be just that: our "brother's keeper." Many obstacles occur along the individual's life journey. Sometimes these bumps in the road lead to discouragement and even deterrence. Sometimes our focus for life is dependent on who others perceive us to be, but becoming who God made us to be should be our primary goal.

Paul said in Ephesians 1:11, "In whom we have obtained an inheritance, being predestinated according to the purpose of Him who worketh all things after the counsel of His own will." When we neglect to adopt God's direction and guidance, we reject the joy and peace that He has promised. When we engage in trailing the paths of the enemy, it is unfortunate because we really do lose a part of ourselves in the process. We are created to care for one another in love. Our responsibility is not to try to stop another's progress, or to participate in any way in the demise or destruction of one another.

An even better way of looking at the scenario is to understand that God chose our roles from the foundation of the world! It behooves each of us to understand that our lives are dependent on who God made us to be. In fact, He simply want us to love each other, which clearly leads to the support of one another. The greatest commandment is stated in Deuteronomy 6:5, We are to "love the Lord thy God with all thine heart, and with all thy soul, and with all thy might." And it is why Jesus restated this important commandment in Matthew 22:39, and followed with, "and the second is like unto it, love your neighbor as yourself!"

June

Genesis 6:6,8, "And it repented the Lord that He had made man on the earth, and it grieved Him at His Heart." "But Noah found grace in the eyes of the Lord."

God's Love: Heart to heart in love. His grace is sufficient.

God's word is true and faithful! Man is created "in the image, and after the likeness" of God. Evidently, God chose man as an extension of Himself. He chose human to human communication for better translation of His Will for life. It is noteworthy for us, human beings, to understand that God could have made some other species His chosen ones, but He gave us a unique glimpse into His Heart, because we are made in His Image. Amazing!

Of all the living things saved after the flood, humans maintained the status of God's loved ones, the chosen of God, who are blessed in the likeness of God, in spite of our disobedience. We continue to fail in our pursuit of living according to the will of God, but He continues to bless us because He **loves** us. He gave us a piece of His Heart! In 2Corinthians 12:9, according to Paul's encounter with his weakness, Jesus said unto him, "my grace is sufficient for thee: for my strength is made perfect in weakness." In other words, regardless of the the situations we face, if we maintain reliance on Christ Jesus, He will bring us out of them.

An old gospel song says it all, "He knows how much we can bear." God's Grace gives us the opportunity to be at peace in the midst of confusion. He gives us His soothing Spirit to combat the sting of pain, horror and dissatisfaction when we need it.

His love for mankind can not be matched no matter how we try. We are sustained by the grace of God because He loves us. He loves us not because of what we do, but by who He made us to be. His love for us is to flow from heart to heart, from His heart to the hearts of His servants.

July

Colossians 3:15 "And let the peace of God rule in your hearts, to the which also ye are called in one body; and be ye thankful."

On one accord: Opportunity for all mankind together in peace.

God the Father specified a particular vision for our lives: God the Son died that we might live out the vision; God the Holy Spirit dwells in us to maintain and sustain our God-installed vision. God, The Father, made provision for humans to receive every possible benefit from His wonderful Grace. He established our hearts to respond to His love in like form, as He had created us. When we allow our hearts to be encompassed with His Glory, we accept that all that we do, we do in honor of God's blessings.

God created this perfect environment so that all men would prosper. He never designated any particular race, creed or color to have superiority over the others. If God had chosen man according to any of the mentioned variables, he probably would have created "that group" in His image, not all humankind. The opportunity for all humans to excel would never have been open to all. He intended for mankind to be just in our interactions with all people.

Colossians 3:17, "And whatsoever ye do in word or deed, do all in the name of the Lord Jesus, giving thanks to God and the Father by him." The opportunity to dwell in peace is open to every one, equally. He expects us to learn to accept one another as sisters and brothers in Christ. As Paul exclaimed in Romans 2:11, "For there is no respect of persons with God." We are given chance after chance to be just in our interaction with each person we encounter. We can achieve the status of having no respect of persons when we decide to approach every one as an equal.

Jesus made it possible for people to live as humans with spiritual expectations. All that we do should be with the expectation of pleasing God as we work to attain the gift of our heavenly home. All things are to be done to glorify God. In the book of John 17:4, Jesus said, " I have glorified thee on the earth. I have finished the work thou gave me." Jesus knew exactly what His goal was, and He never faltered in reaching it. He expects the same of us. His perfect example is our role model.

August

2Chronicles 7:14, "If my people which are called by my name, shall humble themselves, and pray, and seek my face, and turn from their wicked ways, then will I hear from heaven, and will heal their land."

No other love will suffice: It really is God's love and His promise of peace which will heal us all.

It has been asked by some people that, "how can a God allow all the bad stuff in the world?" It has even been asserted that, "God is dead!" But when you really think about it, God has given man multiple opportunities from the beginning of time to turn to Him, to acknowledge Him, to worship Him and to love Him and serve Him as Lord. Many times He instructed His servants to advise the people of His everlasting devotion to them, understand that He and He alone will never forsake them, He will be their God, and protect and provide for them, if they would only trust and obey. The people would be obedient for a short time, then revert to old habits.

This pattern has not changed much over the centuries. We find ourselves in situations of despair and desperation, and no where to turn, then we call on The Lord. As the verse above indicates, Solomon was given specific instructions for the people of God. The same instructions are waiting for us to adopt them now! We, the chosen, His people are to write into our hearts, His Statutes and Commandments, and He will heal our land which He established for us from the beginning, to live in the peace of His Love!

It is imperative that a "Solomon" accept the responsibility to commit to boldly pray for our nation. I believe that any person of faith can be a "Solomon."

In the book of Ecclesiastes 1:9, "The thing that hath been, it is that which shall be done: and there is no new thing under the sun."

If this biblical saying is to be believed, then God has chosen someone who is already anointed for the task. God wants His people to be ready to receive the call.

September

Matthew 11:16, "But whatunto shall I liken this generation? It is like unto children sitting in the markets, and calling unto their fellows, and saying, we have piped unto you, and you have not danced; we have mourned unto you, and ye have not lamented."

Are we really? Will we really hear what thus said the Lord?

Jesus said in Matthew 11:22, "But I say unto you, it shall be more tolerable for Tyre and Sodom at the day of judgment than for you." Could this same message be applicable to us today? I say, it could, indeed. God's word is being preached and taught all across the world, but, it is painfully obvious that too many of us are hearing, but not understanding what's at stake for us as a people.

It is up to those of us who proclaim ourselves "Christian" have the responsibility to compel others to accept Christ as Savior. Many are not yet open to receiving the gospel of truth, and receiving the word as factual. This is simply not a priority for some people. It occurs to this writer that some of our young people are crying, Lamenting for attention. As Matthew 11:15 says, "we have piped unto you." The word has been preached and taught in various ways, but there seems to be a resistance to hearing, a complete lack of interest, and apparently a disconnected thought process when it comes to actually believing that God's word is valid today, just as it was during the times of Abraham, Issac, Jacob and John.

Our children seem to be crying out for guidance, and until we come into the realization that it is crucial to find a way to get the point of God's promise of peace for all, we will perish in our sin!

May I have this dance? Hear the pipe. Well let's dance. Not figuratively, but literally. We must hear the cries of lamentation. Proverbs 29:18, "Where there is no vision, the people perish:" The world is crying out in intense despair, but we continue with business as usual. We say the appropriate things, "oh, that is so sad, I heard something more devastating the other day, when will it stop?" We hear the anguish, we feel the anger and sadness but we must lament! We must repent as a country, as a nation that understands that God will heal this land if only we turn to Him for guidance. We are intended to live in **Peace!**

October

Matthew 6:33, "Seek ye first the kingdom of God, and His righteousness, and all these things shall be added unto you."

Make up your mind: The first commandment for mankind: "Love the Lord our God." Peace comes through the love of God.

It is with intense anticipation that these final devotional months will hopefully be the catalyst to compel any one who has the desire for the truth, those who would want to know more about who God is, to understand what Jesus imparted! Jesus, who actually presented multiple arguments by way of parables, a heavenly message for earthly comprehension. He did it for our benefit.

A God who knew everything about us before our conception, who loved us before we knew who we were, who set each and every aspect of our existence in motion, surely expected us to follow the divine blueprint for life, established from the foundation of the world. What we need most of all is to learn as much as possible about this magnificent God, trust Him, and believe that He is, He was, and, He will always be exactly who He says He is. We will then understand that any thing that we want, and more importantly, anything we need will be supplied by Him.

The only expectation that God has of us is that we allow the Holy Spirit to come in to our hearts and direct us in the fulfillment of His will for our lives. If we can only indulge our hearts in the concept of the "Fruit of the Spirit," we would realize that the entire concept can be accomplished as a whole, in love. This love includes, showing genuine concern for all mankind, protecting one another and generally caring for each other regardless of race, religion, physical or emotional differences. It means being respectful of personal beliefs and understanding that God is no respect of person, and neither should we be.

November

Genesis 1:1, "In the beginning God created the heaven and the earth."

Created for all: He did it for all of us.

The heaven and the earth were created, first for God's purpose and second to define our specific space. God established His Seat in Heaven so that His people would know that we would have His protection at all times. In some gospel songs, and declarations from many believers, "He sits high and looks low." God is in the divine position to watch over us in all that we do. No human being can ascend into heaven to challenge God's position. God's placement of His "Grace and Mercy Seat" is intentional! His Hierarchy is necessary and consistent with His Power to oversee and protect His prized possession, human beings.

The earth is designed to accommodate the lives and the functioning of human life. We have been provided the perfect environment to carry out each and every task assigned to each one of our specifically designed talents. The intent, I believe, is that we would, by the guidance of the Holy Spirit, learn to love each other, regardless of race, religion, sexual orientation, or any of the multiple variables that make us different. We are one people in the sight of God. The path has been established through the word of God. Yes, we are given free will, but a degree of responsibility comes with this freedom of will that should be adopted by any person made in the image/after the likeness of God.

I agree there are aspects of our lives that are abominations to God, but, God also reminds us in His Word, Romans 12:9, that "vengeance is mine." None of us are in a position to condemn or judge another. The Word of God is based on the Heart of God. The heart of God is the love of God. He knew we would have variable opinions and interpretations of His Inspired Word, but He expected us to remain respectful and understanding of each one's views without malice or disdain. We will not all agree, but in Christ we must love one another. It should never be a major undertaking to love a brother or sister as God loves us, in spite of our multiple differences and specific ethnic mores. God's love for us is never ending, and His expectation for His people is that we understand His desire for our peace in a land of multi-cultural ideas and experiences.

Based on the Word of God, in the examples presented in the Holy Bible, everything comes down to love, which implies dignity, respect and consideration for one another. God's love for us is beyond measure. If we could only realize that God can change the course of our lives at any time. Think back to the story of Noah in Genesis 6:7, "And the Lord said, I will destroy man whom I have created from the face of the earth; both man, and beast, and the creeping thing, and the fowls of the air; for it repented Me that I have made them." Reading this verse is actually chilling, but read on in verse 8: "But Noah found grace in the eyes of the Lord."

We too are still here for a purpose! We too can find grace in the eyes of the Lord!

December:

Acts 13:22-23, "And when He had removed him, He raised up unto them David to be their King; to whom also He gave testimony, and said, I have found David the son of Jesse, a man after Mine Own Heart, which shall fulfill all my will. Of this man's seed hath God according to His Promise raised unto Israel a Saviour, Jesus."

He only wants the best for all: The peace of Man's heart is God's.

The motivation of a man's mind is expressed from the depths of his heart. When God declared David a man after His own heart, it provided us an insight into who God expects us to be.

He knows that we will fall into temptation and despair without vile or malicious intent.

A man's mind reveals the content of his heart. The heart of a man is that part God values most. It is important to understand that no human being is capable of reading another's heart. This ability is uniquely God's alone. If we could read one another's heart, chaos and division would be never-ending. There would never be peace because our time would be spent defending our thoughts.

Our peace in this life is totally dependent on our relationship with God who has designed our minds to depend on The Lord Jesus for all our needs.

Paul describes Jesus' provision of hope for us in Philippians 4:13, when he writes, "I can do all things through Christ which strengthens me." The peace of Jesus allows us to weather any storm. Major changes occur in our lives, some which we have no control over, like weather-related, and then some are of our own making, personal and collectively. In spite of the difficulties, we are still here. We are given multiple opportunities to reassess and reset our hearts and minds in the direction of God-led principles and performance. It is never too late to start over! When we awake and are able to function, it is right on time. David was not perfect by any means, but he remembered the importance of repentance and renewal.

Paul, The greatest Apostle, wanted the truth of the gospel to reach every heart. He expected those to whom he ministered to use his example as a guide. In Philippians 4:9, "Those things, which you have both learned, and received, and heard, and seen in me, do. And the God of peace shall be with you." If we could only remember that God ordains each and every one of us for peace, love and joy. God gifted each of us with a special task, and He prepares us to perform.

Ephesians 2:10, "For we are His workmanship, created in Christ Jesus unto good works, which God hath before ordained that we should walk in them."

Some of us hesitate to walk into our gifts, and some of us ignore them altogether, while others are determined to emphatically fulfill our calling, but none of us are left to our own. This is the month that we commemorate the birth of Jesus, an excellent time for renewal and repentance.

Isaiah 26:3, "Thou will keep him in perfect peace, whose mind is stayed on thee:"

Our peace comes through the Grace of God in Jesus Christ.

Voice D. Jones Guy
Memphis, Tennessee 38128
(901) 569-0203
G_voice@bellsouth.net

Hospice Nurse
Write short stories, plays and speeches
Church Musician

"My Peace I Leave With You"

*T*he concept of peace may be an illusion for some of us, but there is hope through the sacrifice of our Lord and Savior, Jesus Christ who has left us the blueprint for life. Answers to all our concerns are written in the Holy Bible. Recalling the term peace in my study of the Word Of God, it occurs to me that God's intent for all mankind, His prized possession, is for us to be happy and content as we strive for perfection in our multi-designated tasks.

He gave us all that we need to accomplish our many goals, beginning with our interpretation of the family establishment. It is imperative that we understand our purpose in relation to the family. When there is peace in the family, peace will follow in individual lives. When we are taught basic concepts of peace and respect in the home, we carry them over into all aspects of our lives. Even if we run off course, we can reclaim previously taught perspectives and re-establish our standing to

be examples for others. God designed the family unit to nurture, direct and instruct in the ways of the Lord. God set everything in order to work for us, so that we would have the greatest chance of succeeding in the perfectly peaceful environment which He created just for us.

In the book of Isaiah 54:13, "And all thy children shall be taught of the Lord; and great shall be the peace of thy children."

Citations

1. John 5:36
2. John 5:24
3. John 5:30
4. Mark 6:3; Matthew 13:55;
5. Matthew 27:27-43
6. Jeremiah 29:10-14
7. Jeremiah 29:10-14
8. Matthew 5: 20-48
9. 2 Corinthians 1:17-24
10. Exodus 29:28, Leviticus 20:24, Numbers 6:14
11. Matthew 17:20
12. Sermon from Pastor Alton R. Williams
13. Matthew 26:45
14. Mark 4:33-34
15. Luke 24:45-48
16. Luke 24:44-45
17. Matthew 10:1-42
18. Mark 1:9-11
19. John 4:27-30
20. John 4:1-54
21. Galatians 5:22-26
22. Words of 105 year old woman
23. Acts 1:1-9
24. Images from "Pixabay free image site"

The author's perspective and interpretation in studying the word of God.